JUST LOOK AT...

LIVING
IN THE DESERT

JUST LOOK AT...
LIVING IN THE DESERT

John Cloudsley-Thompson

Rourke Enterprises, Inc.
Vero Beach, FL 32964

Factual Adviser: Dr Andrew Warren
University College London

Editor: Nicole Lagneau
Teacher Panel: Tim Firth,
Stephen Harley, Lynn McCoombe
Designer: Ewing Paddock
Production: Rosemary Bishop
Picture Research: Caroline Mitchell

Illustrations
Mike Atkinson 10–11, 16–17, 34–35, 43
Ann Baum 12–13, 14–15, 21, 22, 25,
26–27, 28, 36–37, 38, 40–41.
Susan Neale back cover, 9, 12, 24, 25,
26, 42

Photographs
Aldus Archive/Royal Geographical Society,
18T & B
Aldus Archive/Shell, 22–23
Camerapix Hutchison Library, 23, 29T & B,
32–33T
Professor John Cloudsley-Thompson, 32
Bruce Coleman, 13
Daily Telegraph Colour Library, 8–9B, 20
Robert Harding Picture Library, 8B, 15, 19,
20–21B, 25, 30, 33B, 34T & B
Christine Osborne, cover, 30–31, 38
Spectrum Colour Library, 10
ZEFA, title page, 8–9T, 11, 16–17, 20–21T, 37,
39

How to use this book

Look first in the contents page to see if the subject you want is listed. For instance, if you want to find out about nomads you will find the information on pages 14 and 15. The word list explains the more difficult terms found in this book. The index will tell you how many times a particular subject is mentioned and whether there is a picture of it.

Living in the Desert is one of a series of books on how people live. All the books on this subject have an orange color band around the cover. If you want to know more about how people live, look for other books with an orange color band in the **Just Look At. . .** series.

Library of Congress Cataloging in Publication Data

Cloudsley-Thompson, J. L.
  Living in the desert.

  (Just look at . . .)
  Includes index.
  Summary: Discusses the people, animals, and plants of the desert areas of the world, as well as problems of deserts and ways man is trying to deal with them.
  1. Deserts—Juvenile literature.   2. Desert ecology—Juvenile literature.   3. Desert resources development—Juvenile literature. [1. Deserts.   2. Desert ecology]
I. Title. II. Series.
GB611.C59 1985   304.2'5   85-14370
ISBN 0-86592-911-4

Contents

onument Valley in Arizona,
S.A. is one of the wonders
the world. The weird and
xtraordinary shapes of
cks or buttes are remains
rocky hills.

PEOPLE OF THE DESERT

Nearly one fifth of the land surface of the world is occupied by hot deserts and semi-desert regions. Deserts are dry, barren places which receive scanty, irregular rainfall. However, where there is water, deserts are extremely rich and fertile. The banks of rivers and oases are the places in which most of the inhabitants live. Several of the earliest human civilizations first began to develop in oases on the banks of rivers, such as the Nile, Indus, Tigris and Euphrates.

Most deserts lie near the tropics, north and south of the equator. Death Valley in California, and parts of the Sahara Desert are the hottest places on Earth during the daytime. However, at night, especially in the winter, they become quite cool. Further from the equator, the Gobi desert can be horribly cold and windy in winter, even though it is extremely hot in summer. The regions around the North and South Poles are known as "cold" or "polar" deserts.

In this book we shall only be talking about hot deserts and the different ways of life and cultures of the people who live in them. The modern city dwellers of Arizona can buy the luxury provided by modern technology while hunters and gatherers of the Namib and Australian deserts scratch a bare living from the land. In between these two extremes, farmers and traders live settled lives in oases.

◄ The desert can be very fertile when water flows into it. On the far left, water irrigates winter wheat in the Gobi desert.

On the left, shepherds in eastern Iran move around to find pasture and water for their sheep and goats.

This Botswana bushman of the Kalahari desert is shooting a poisoned arrow with his bow. A quiver to hold other arrows is slung over his shoulder, and strings of seeds decorate his legs. ►

An American Desert

The deserts of the world cover large areas, but few people live in them because the environment is so harsh. However, with the help of modern technology the people of the desert city of Phoenix, Arizona, have managed to make their lives very comfortable.

A luxurious life

The wealthy people who live in Phoenix have air-conditioned cars in air-conditioned garages, and drive to air-conditioned shops, restaurants or movies. They do not have to get out of their cars when they go home because the garage doors are operated by remote control. They have air-conditioned houses and offices. They nearly all have pools in their luxurious gardens. The public swimming baths are large enough to contain machines that make artificial waves for people who like surf riding.

▲ Phoenix is a very modern city in Arizona. It is surrounded by desert, and all its water comes from wells. The distant hills are bare rock, and very little vegetation grows on them.

Air conditioner

Water Shortage

All these things use up a great deal of energy, which comes from oil. They use up precious water too. Phoenix and Tucson in Arizona, like the desert cities of New Mexico, California and Texas, depend largely upon sources of water that are not being replaced. This water comes from wells, dug deep in the ground.

When the wells dry up, life in the cities will not be possible unless water can be brought to them. The water in the wells is mostly "fossil water". This means that it comes from rain that fell during the ice ages, hundreds of thousands of years ago. Not enough rain falls in the desert today to refill the wells.

The human population of the southwestern states of America has increased greatly during the last thirty years. So people use a great deal more water than in the past. They need it to water their fields for instance. However, so much water has been taken from the Colorado River that the river no longer runs into the sea in Mexico. Over the years, it has become more and more difficult for some people to earn a living from the land.

Navajo houses are built of dried mud. They are attractive to look at and surprisingly comfortable.

Navajo Indians

Some of the Indians of the Navajo tribe who live in the deserts around Phoenix and Tucson have adapted themselves to the American way of life. At the same time, they are trying to preserve their own customs and run their own affairs. Most of these people are unskilled workers and cannot afford the luxuries of modern technology. They earn a living by weaving and making handicrafts for sale to tourists. On the Indian reservations the soil is poor and life is difficult. The Navajo Indians do not feel that their rights are being fully recognized by the government. Would they have a better life if they abandoned their ancient tribal way of life?

Solar panels

This modern home in Phoenix is equipped with solar panels on the roof to produce electricity. It is air-conditioned, and has every modern luxury.

Hunters and Gatherers

Some desert dwellers live on what they can hunt and gather in the desert. They have to live on what they can find in their immediate environment: edible plants, fruit and game. Today, these people are found only in two of the world's deserts. The San people or Bushmen live in the Namib and Kalahari region of southern Africa, and the Bindibu Aboriginals in the Australian desert. They plant no crops, have no settled homes, and keep no domesticated animals except dogs.

Bushmen are excellent hunters. They can hit a moving antelope with a poisoned arrow from a distance of over 400 feet. The women and children use grubbing sticks to dig the earth for edible bulbs and roots. Tsama melons are especially prized for the water they hold. Bushmen have to be very careful to save water at all times. They wear few clothes. At night they rest in temporary shelters. These are made from the skins of wild animals which are laid across the branches of thorn trees.

A Bushwoman is drinking water from an ostrich shell. Water is very precious in the desert. Bushmen store it in gourds and empty ostrich shells.

Here you see a San lady carrying her baby. Around her waist is a bag of roots and groundnuts that she has collected. In her right hand she carries the forked-grubbing stick which she uses for digging the earth in search of food.

▲ These rock paintings were made by Bushmen in the Kalahari desert, in Botswana. Rock paintings show the importance of art in their lives.

Aborigines

The Australian Aborigines of the Bindibu tribes live in much the same way as do the Bushmen. They, too, are extremely skillful at tracking game, which they kill with spears and boomerangs. Boomerangs are throwing sticks. They are shaped like a new moon. When they are thrown they follow a curved path through the air. Aborigines make two kinds of boomerang. Small ones are used for sport. These make a complete circle and return to the thrower. Larger boomerangs do not return, although they follow a curved path. They are used for hunting and warfare.

While the men are out hunting, their wives and children trudge long distances every day to collect edible roots, bulbs, and firewood. The Aborigines have to camp near water. They have no melons or ostrich eggs in which to carry water. Their shelters are no more than windbreaks made of sticks or clumps of grass. When moving around, they carry lighted fire sticks which are used to start new camp fires.

▲ The Australian Aborigine is making himself a new spear. He is using his teeth to pull the bark from a long stick. Afterward he will sharpen the point, so that he can use it to hunt.

Fires are very important, not only for cooking but to keep their naked bodies warm at night. Aborigines make daily trips into the desert from one water hole to another to collect food. They have few possessions. They leave their grinding stones and platters, ready for use, at each camp site. There is nobody to steal them as each tribe has its own territory. Some people may carry water bags made of kangaroo skins, or painted baskets made from the bark of trees. They use stone tools and sew with needles made from bone.

The Aborigines believe that each tribe or clan is descended from a particular plant or animal, which must be protected by magic ceremonies. Like the San Bushmen, most of the Australian Aboriginals have now abandoned their ancient ways of life. Some of them have become laborers on cattle or sheep ranches. Others live as farmers on the fringes of towns and villages. Many depend upon social security and unemployment benefits because their old way of life has disappeared.

Nomads

In places where rain falls at intervals of several years, human beings can survive only by using the habits of the nomads. They have to keep moving around in search of pasture and water for their animals.

Until recently, some of the Tubu of the eastern Sahara used to wander in small groups, with a few camels and goats, over hundreds of miles of almost lifeless country. In the places where they lived, the rain falls on average only once in thirty to fifty years! People say, in jest, that a Tubu can live for three days on one date: the first on its skin, the second on its pulp and the third on its kernel. The Tubu also collect edible grasses, and grind the fruits of the dom palm to make flour. The Tubu live in desert that is too harsh to support large herds.

▲ The Mongolian winters are very cold although the summers are extremely hot. The tents, or yurts, are made of thick felt for warmth. They can easily be taken down when the tribes move from one place to another.

Water

Rain does not fall regularly in desert regions and is unreliable. Torrents may fall in one place while, a little further away, there is no rain at all. In Cairo, Egypt, there is often no rain for a year or more but, in one storm about fifty years ago, buses and trains were sunk in mud up to the level of their windows. The houses of unbaked-mud bricks melted away like lumps of sugar. The rain from desert storms is usually wasted because it runs off the ground so soon that there is not enough time for it to soak into the soil. It disappears down deep water courses that are dry most of the time.

In Africa and the Middle East these dry water courses are known as *wadis* while, in America, they are called *arroyos*. The sun, blazing down from a cloudless sky, quickly dries up the desert after every shower. Even so, after a heavy storm plants burst into life and fresh green grass sprouts from the desert sand.

Falconry is a favorite sport among Arab sheiks. Falcons must be tamed and carefully trained. The owner wears a thick muff so that the sharp talons of his hawk will not cut into his flesh.

▲ This a Bedouin tent. It is made of cloth woven from goat hair. The interior is separated into two halves, one for the women, in which all the cooking is done, the other for the men. The tent can be moved in pieces and loaded onto camels when the people move on to new pastures.

Bedouin and Tuareg

Where there is more vegetation, people can move about in larger groups with bigger flocks and herds, like the Bedouin of North Africa and the Middle East, the Tuareg, and the Mongol tribesmen of the Karakum desert in Central Asia. People of the Bedouin tribes originally came from Arabia. They are mostly camel herders, and live in tents made of goats' hair. In the Sahara, they live alongside the Tuareg, who were the original Berber inhabitants of the great desert. Tuareg culture is different from that of the Bedouin. The men wear flowing blue robes. They keep the sand from their nostrils with veils of black or indigo-blue cloth.

The Tuareg live mainly on milk from their herds. They move with their large flocks and herds from one thin pasture to another, going to the places where the rain falls every year. Each dry season they return to the same wells. It is a difficult life. The Tuareg have few material goods apart from their camels, sheep and goats. Their tents and everything else they possess, have to be carried on the backs of camels or donkeys. In recent years the Bedouin and Tuareg have suffered terribly in the Sahel desert drought.

▲ Tuareg men of northern Niger are dancing during one of their religious festivals. As they stamp with their feet, the dust rises up from the desert soil. Festivals are one of the many customs preserved by desert people over hundreds of years.

Oasis Dwellers

Some of the most productive and thickly cultivated places in the world can be found in deserts. These are the oases. Many of them are quite small. Others cover hundreds of square miles. In some of them are important cities whose inhabitants have developed special ways for cultivating their crops.

Resting places

Most of the oases of Africa were first used as resting places on the long caravan routes across the desert. Here the merchants would halt their strings of camels. The animals would be given unlimited food and water for a few days. This refreshed them so that they would be ready to cross the next expanse of empty wilderness. Later, people began to live permanently in desert oases. Flourishing markets sprang up and goods were exchanged.

This dome shaped building in the Iranian desert is an old ice house, built before the day of refrigerators. During the cold winter nights a thin film of ice formed on the surface of the shallow pool on the right. The following morning the ice was shovelled through a small door into the ice house where it was stored. Although some melted, and the water trickled away, enough remained to make ices and cool drinks in the summer. ▶

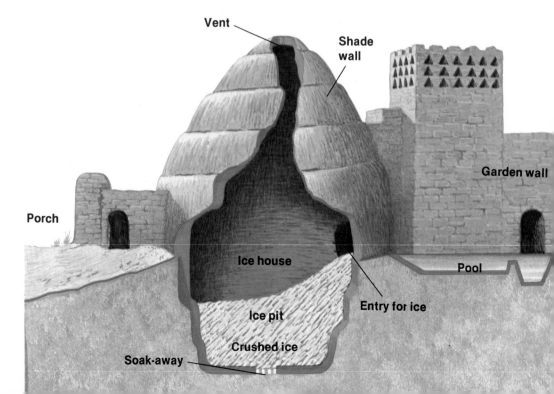

Vent

Shade wall

Garden wall

Porch

Ice house

Pool

Entry for ice

Ice pit

Crushed ice

Soak-away

16

◀ The oasis of El-Oued in Algeria, with the date palms on which the people depend for their livelihood. The young trees are planted in deep holes to bring them closer to the ground water.

Crops

Date palms provide the most important product of the oases of African deserts. Underneath the palm trees a variety of valuable crops are grown. These include lemons and figs, olives, grapes, apricots, pomegranates, guavas, wheat, maize, millet, beans, peas, onions, tomatoes, sweet potatoes and spices. The inhabitants of the oases work hard to prevent the drifting sand from blowing over their plantations. They keep out the sand with complex patterns of fences made of palm leaves.

Keeping cool

In some of the oases of Iran, great cities have flourished for 6,000 years or more on the edge of the desert. The houses of Iranian towns are dominated by mud brick towers which look like large chimneys. These are wind catchers which bring drafts of fresh, dry air into the living rooms. Although this air is hot, it helps to evaporate sweat. In the intense heat of summer, wind catchers make life much more comfortable indoors.

Oases

Some oases depend for their water upon natural sources of water, such as springs, and wells. Many of the oases of North Africa are beside springs. Other oases draw their waters from rivers entering the desert. These rivers flow from nearby mountains where there is heavy rainfall or snow. Oases of this kind are found on the fringes of the Karakum desert, at Sinkiang in China, and along the foothills of the Andes mountains. Green ribbons of cultivated land occur all along the banks of the Indus, Tigris, Euphrates, Colorado, Rio Grande and other desert rivers. The Nile valley is the largest oasis in the world.

◀ The houses of Iran are designed to catch the wind. In this diagram, the red lines show how the wind circulates through wind-catchers and down into the living rooms of the house. This makes life much more comfortable indoors during the hot summer.

Wind direction

Vents

Cut-away section of tower

Sun

Wind tower

Shade

Living room

Explorers

From the earliest times people have been fascinated by the cultures and ways of life of desert people. There are several reasons for this. The desert landscape is mysterious, and often extremely beautiful. Some desert explorers have travelled in search of gold. The Spanish Conquerors did so in Mexico and Peru in the 1500's. Other explorers have been scientists. A few have gone in search for peace and quiet or to escape from a life they did not like. They must all have experienced heat, thirst and discomfort and even lost their lives. Most explorers went in search of adventure. Before there were trucks and cars, desert travelers had to ride on the backs of camels.

Camel caravans
Camels carried tents, food and water. Caravans followed regular routes from oasis to oasis. It is dangerous and stupid to travel alone in the desert unless you keep to regular routes. If your car breaks down or your camel gets lame, you may die within a day when the water runs out. Explorers never leave the beaten track without taking at least two vehicles, and large reserves of water.

▲ Gertrude Bell, the famous British woman explorer, is about to set off on her travels. From the age of 30, she spent most of her time in the Near East desert.

◄ This photograph, taken by Gertrude, shows some Arabs making coffee for their guests. Although great changes have taken place, traditional hospitality has not changed in Arab homes. Guests are always welcomed and invited to join in the coffee ceremony.

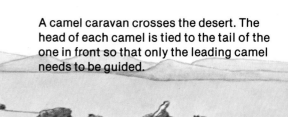

A camel caravan crosses the desert. The head of each camel is tied to the tail of the one in front so that only the leading camel needs to be guided.

Even so, fatal accidents sometimes happen. Early this century, a caravan of several hundred people and camels died in the Sahara, and many other people have died when they got lost or their cars broke down.

European Explorers

Disguised as an Arab, Sir Richard Burton went on a pilgrimage to Mecca in 1853. he was one of the first Europeans to do so. A year later, he was the first to enter Harar. This was a forbidden city in the desert, in the eastern part of Ethiopia. Another famous explorer was Gertrude Bell. From the age of 30, Gertrude spent most of her time in the Near East desert. In 1913, she set out on an historic journey from Damascus to Ha'il in Arabia.

Camels have the advantage that they do not get stuck in the sand. They do not have to be dug out and pushed like wheeled vehicles. ▼

On the way, she and her guides were attacked by a group of shepherds armed with swords and rifles. Gertrude kept calm. Luckily, the shepherds' leaders, who knew the guides, rode up and made the shepherds give back everything they had stolen. Later, Gertrude crossed the orange sand dunes of the Great Nafud where no European had ventured before.

Heinrich Barth

One of the longest desert expeditions was that of the German Heinrich Barth. Early in 1850, Barth set out from Tripoli, in Libya, on a British expedition with James Richardson and Adolf Olweg. He explored the desert around Lake Chad, reached Timbuktu on the river Niger and returned across the Sahara to Tripoli. He wrote five large books filled with important information about the Sahara and its people.

A great dune of silvery sand beside a hill of black rock in eastern Iran. Rock and stone take up greater areas of desert throughout the world than sand does.

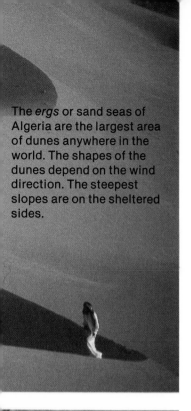

The *ergs* or sand seas of Algeria are the largest area of dunes anywhere in the world. The shapes of the dunes depend on the wind direction. The steepest slopes are on the sheltered sides.

DESERT LANDS

Most people think of a desert as a vast region of drifting sand, without vegetation except for an occasional oasis. This is true of some, but by no means typical of all desert regions. Sometimes the desert is a rocky plateau, sometimes it is a pebbly plain. In some places, there are sand seas with huge dunes. Ther are three main types of desert, sandy deserts or *ergs*, rocky deserts or *hammada*, and stony deserts or *reg*. Deserts can be made in different ways but they are always formed because there is not enough water.

The two bands of desert in the hottest part of the world, north and south of the equator, are called tropical deserts. In these warm areas, clouds carrying rain are not brought to these deserts. The Sahara and Kalahari deserts for example, are tropical deserts. Other places are deserts because they are too far from the sea to get much rain. Such deserts are found in the middle of continents, in Central Asia for instance.

Sometimes mountains prevent the winds from dropping their moisture. This creates rain shadow deserts. They include the Mojave and Great Basin deserts of North America and the Patagonian desert. Cool currents along the coast of South Africa have produced coastal deserts such as the Namib and Atacama. The cool winds which blow over these currents cannot hold much moisture. Such deserts are often foggy but they seldom get any rain.

◄ Qaski women milking goats in the stony desert of Mongolia.

The four main types of sand dune. *Seif* is an Arabic word meaning sword and seif dunes look like rows of swords lying beside one another. ►

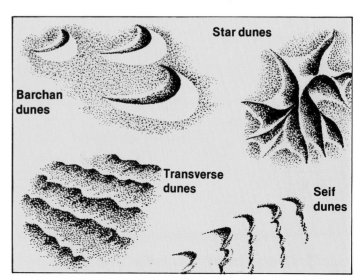

Barchan dunes

Star dunes

Transverse dunes

Seif dunes

Sandstorms occur in desert regions, because there are so few plant roots to bind the soil together. Each year between 60 and 200 million tons of dust are blown from the Sahara into the Atlantic Ocean. ▶

Hazards

The lack of water in the desert affects all living things. When it does rain, there are floods and torrents. The tremendous change in temperature from day to night affects people and animals alike.

Small animals such as jerboas and kangaroo rats hide in holes during the day to keep away from the heat. They come out at night when it is cooler. It is hard to imagine how harsh a desert wind can be when there is nowhere to shelter. It is even worse when the wind brings a sand storm with it. Then it cakes you with yellow mud, spoils your food, and stops you from seeing anything. In one sand storm, in Libya, you could not see an electric light at night from five paces away.

Diseases

Climate is not the only problem of people who live in deserts. Insects, too, make life difficult. Flies can be an absolute pest and they help spread many diseases such as trachoma and dysentery. In much of North Africa, well over half the oasis dwellers suffer from trachoma, an eye disease spread by flies. Many sufferers are left partially or completely blind as a result. Sandfly fever is transmitted by sandflies. These tiny, biting insects are very common in some desert regions. Parts of the Great Australian Desert are plagued by fleas which suck the blood of travelers.

Human diseases are widespread in the oases of the underdeveloped countries of the world, because too many people live close together in unhealthy conditions. Of these diseases, malaria kills most people. It is passed on by mosquitoes which breed in oasis water. Small fishes were introduced from Texas in 1926, into the lakes and ponds of Algeria. They fed on mosquito larvae and gradually helped to rid many oases of malaria. However, the disease keeps returning.

Bilharzia is one of the most dreadful diseases of tropical oases. It is caused by a small organism called a blood fluke. These flukes spend part of their life cycle in a fresh water snail, and part in the human body. The larvae from the snails burrow through the skin. People become infected when padding, washing, or drinking. The snails become infected when the sick person urinates in the water.

Desert locust

▲ A swarm of locusts in the Negev desert of Israel. The desert locust (box) can be recognized by its striped eyes. Both desert and migratory locusts plague the Sahara and the deserts of the Middle East.

▲ Locusts are grasshoppers which normally live in green vegetation on the desert's edge. When their numbers build up, they form great swarms which are thick enough to darken the skies.

The disease is difficult to control because it is almost impossible to prevent small children from bathing when the weather is hot. The cure is also unpleasant.

Pests

There a great many valuable crops in the oases. These are protected by the surrounding desert. The desert acts as a barrier to the introduction of plant pests and diseases because it has few plants and therefore few pests. However, once they have been introduced, these pests and diseases flourish. Various kinds of scale insects are important pests of date palms. One of them was introduced into the Sahara from Egypt centuries ago. It is still accidentally being spread from one oasis to another. It has not yet reached Chad or the southwestern oases, although it is now found in Algeria and Morocco.

Desert locusts are carried long distances by wind. They are taken into the upper air and come down where rain is likely to fall. In this way they are able to cross vast areas of barren desert. They reach oases and regions where the local people plant crops. The female locust lays her eggs in damp sand. After the young hoppers hatch, they feed on the grass that springs up after the rain. When they have grown up, their wings are formed and they fly away in swarms in search of food.

Vegetation

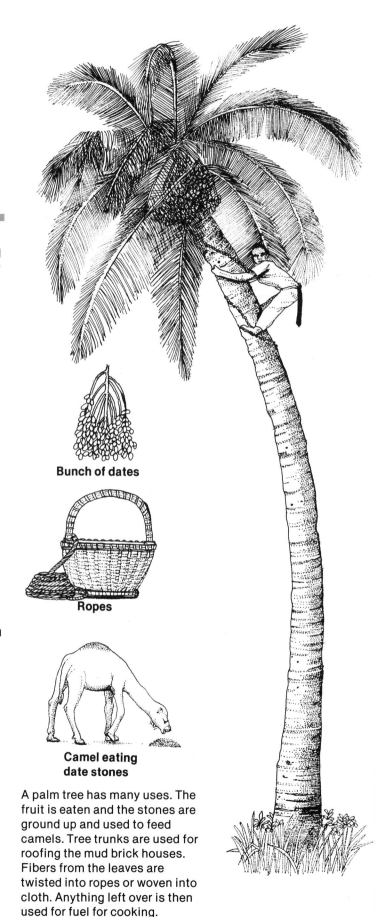

The desert changes completely after a rainstorm. The seeds of grasses and other small herbs spring into life as soon as the rain comes. They grow very quickly so that, within a day or two, the desert becomes green. This does not last for long. The blazing sun and scorching winds soon dry up the ground. The vegetation turns brown and disappears.

The grasses and small herbs have very short lifecycles. They flower, set seed, and die within three or four weeks. They are able to live in the desert because they are active only when moisture is available. They pass the rest of the time as dry seeds, which are not killed by the heat and drought. Such plants are sometimes called "ephemerals" because their lifecycles are so brief.

Life in the desert
The green leaves of new plants are soon gobbled up by locusts, grasshoppers and caterpillars. All these insects provide welcome food for scorpions, spiders and camel spiders. Birds which migrate appear and build their nests. Snakes, lizards, jerboas, kangaroo rats, ground squirrels, and foxes produce their young while there is plenty of food available.

Nomads, such as Tubu and Tuareg, come in search of new pasture for their camels, sheep and goats. When all the grass has been eaten or withered away, they move off in search of grazing elsewhere.

Climate and plants
The Sahara, Arabian, Indian, and other sub-tropical deserts get rain in summer. Tropical rain which falls in the heat of the summer is known as "monsoon" rain. It is always welcome.

Bunch of dates

Ropes

Camel eating date stones

A palm tree has many uses. The fruit is eaten and the stones are ground up and used to feed camels. Tree trunks are used for roofing the mud brick houses. Fibers from the leaves are twisted into ropes or woven into cloth. Anything left over is then used for fuel for cooking.

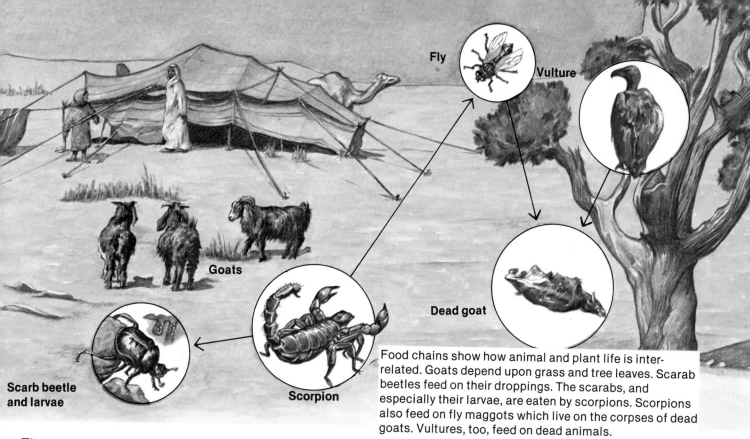

Fly

Vulture

Goats

Dead goat

Scarb beetle and larvae

Scorpion

Food chains show how animal and plant life is inter-related. Goats depend upon grass and tree leaves. Scarab beetles feed on their droppings. The scarabs, and especially their larvae, are eaten by scorpions. Scorpions also feed on fly maggots which live on the corpses of dead goats. Vultures, too, feed on dead animals.

The monsoon winds which bring rain each year to deserts between the tropics are particularly important in India where so many people depend upon them. When the monsoon fails, their crops wither and the people starve.

Large parts of the desert are not completely barren between rainstorms. Except in moving sand dunes and rocky deserts, there is usually some permanent vegetation. This is concentrated on the banks of *wadis* and *arroyos*. Permanent desert vegetation consists of clumps of grasses which last through the year, and trees. The trees have extremely long roots which reach down to water far below the desert surface. Some African desert acacias, have been found with roots to a depth of over 45 feet.

Other plants which can resist drought may have shallow roots which collect water after every downpour. The water is stored by cacti and euphorbias, another type of desert plant, in their fleshy stems. These swell up when there is plenty of water, and shrink in times of drought.

The desert environment is very similar in every part of the world. Euphorbias and cacti are not closely related but they look alike because they are affected by the desert in the same way. Euphorbias are found in Africa but cacti come from America. ▶

Saguaro Cactus

Euphorbia **Cactus**

Namib Euphorbia

Wild Animals

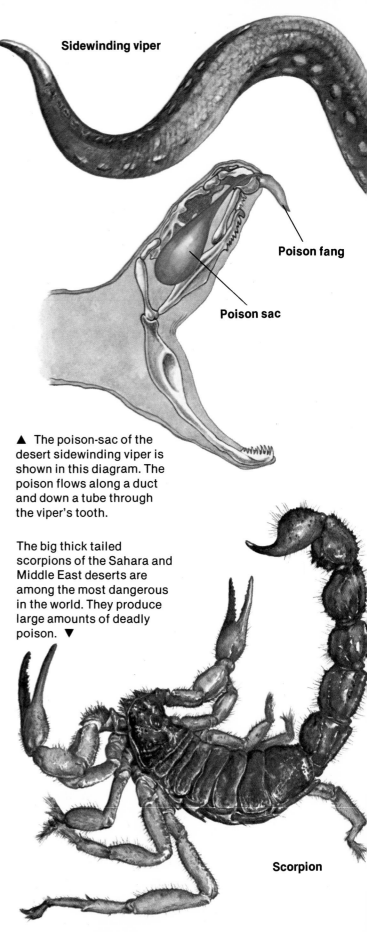

Sidewinding viper

Poison fang

Poison sac

Some people are afraid of the desert because of the poisonous animals that live there. Desert scorpions are the most poisonous of all scorpions, but the chances of getting stung are slight, especially if you are careful. Scorpions use their poison to kill insect prey and only sting people who hurt them by mistake. The poison of some kinds of scorpion is dangerous, but most can only cause pain. Some scorpions hiss when they are disturbed and this warns people to leave them alone.

Camel spiders are very strong for their size. Most kinds are bigger than real spiders and have long legs. They are very hairy and run so fast that they look like balls of thistledown blowing across the desert. They feed on insects and scorpions and are extremely greedy, but they are not poisonous.

▲ The poison-sac of the desert sidewinding viper is shown in this diagram. The poison flows along a duct and down a tube through the viper's tooth.

The big thick tailed scorpions of the Sahara and Middle East deserts are among the most dangerous in the world. They produce large amounts of deadly poison. ▼

Scorpion

▲ The ostrich is the only desert bird that does not have to shade its eggs from the midday sun. The eggs are big enough not to get overheated. At dusk and during the night the ostrich sits on them to make them hatch.

▲ The sidewinding viper moves in a peculiar way, leaving a row of grooves in the sand.

Snakes

Most snakes are harmless and become quite tame if they are treated kindly. Even poisonous kinds kill their prey and do not bite humans unless they are disturbed or hurt. Vipers and cobras usually warn people to keep away from them by hissing. Rattlesnakes make an angry buzzing noise by shaking their rattles. These are made of horny pieces of dry skin at the end of the tail. It would be very bad luck to be bitten by a poisonous snake, but there is little need to be frightened. The most dangerous animal in the world is the mosquito. Many more people die from malaria than from all the other bites and stings put together!

Plants and animals

Biologists are interested in all the plants and animals of the desert. Hunters and nomads usually only care about the ones that harm them, or which they can eat. The animals they hunt in the deserts of Asia and Africa are ostriches, gazelles and antelopes. These are now becoming rather scarce. In Australia, the Aborigines hunt kangaroos and wallabies.

The pronghorn antelopes used to be hunted by the Indians of the American deserts. They are now rare. The largest antelopes of the Sahara and Arabian deserts are oryx antelopes. Oryx are formidale creatures when annoyed. Their horns are long and sharp, and they scream through their noses when they charge. Oryx can exist without drinking. They get enough water from their food. The leaves of acacia trees and roots can provide them with enough food.

Gazelles, too, seldom drink, and travel long distances to get water. The addax antelope is smaller and weaker than the oryx. It can live on even drier vegetation. So it lives in even more remote parts of the Sahara. The odd looking saiga antelope roams the plains of Western Asia.

Several kinds of wild donkeys are found in the deserts of Africa and Asia. These surefooted animals can go without water for a long time. When they do drink, however, they are able to take in relatively much more water than a human being could.

Addax

Oryx

▲ The oryx antelope has long sharp horns and is safe from most enemies except humans. The addax has spiral horns. It is weaker than the oryx, but lives in more barren deserts where its enemies cannot reach it.

Camels, Sheep and Goats

The camel is the most important animal of the nomads. There are two kinds of camel. The dromedary has a single hump. It is found in Arabia, India and North Africa. The bactrian camel inhabits the deserts of central Asia where the winters are very cold. It has shorter legs and its winter coat is longer and darker. The dromedary was first used as a working animal about 4,000 years ago. It became domesticated. There are no wild single humped camels any more. However, there are still herds of wild bactrian camels in the Gobi desert. In Australia, there are wild dromedaries. They were imported into the country. There are so many that they are now classed as "vermin".

Camels

Camels are calm creatures. When treated kindly, they work hard and travel very long distances across the desert. They know exactly how heavy their loads should be, and refuse to move if they are overloaded. The camel can live for several days without drinking or eating. The hump is a food reserve and contains fat. This food reserve is used up in the dry season when there is little vegetation to eat.

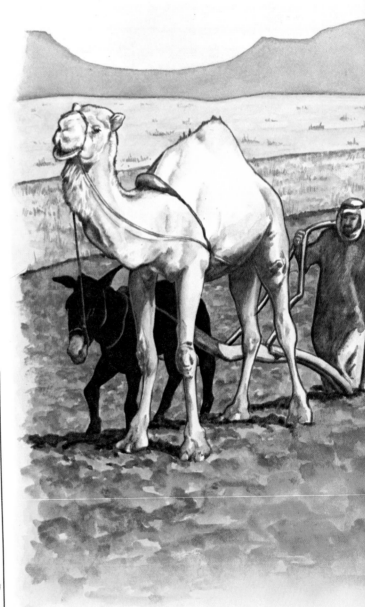

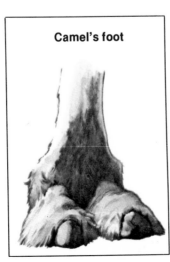

Camel's foot

Camels are descended from animals like llamas and alpacas which did not live in desert. Like cows and sheep, their ancestors had only two toes on each foot. The fleshy pads on the camel's toes prevent its feet from sinking into the desert sand. Camels are used for all kinds of work. They carry people and goods, pull carts and even plows.

▲ Camels, goats and sheep are being given water at a well in Niger. Camels do not need to drink as often as sheep and goats. They can, therefore, graze further afield.

▲ In the cold winters of the Mongolian deserts, and in the Himalayas, the yak is used as a beast of burden. It provides good milk and meat. Its long hair is woven into cloth for making clothes and tents.

Camels do not sweat as much as we do. We lose water when we sweat. Camels store heat during the day, and cool off during the night. They do not begin to sweat until they are really overheated. In this way they save precious water.

Cattle

Nomadic shepherds who do not grow plants for their food depend upon their domesticated animals. They drive the animals out from the villages to graze each day in the countryside. In very dry regions, only camels and goats can survive. Where there is more grass and water, people also own sheep and cattle. The Indians of the Atacama and Peruvian desert regions have llamas and alpacas. These are relatives of the camels which live in the Andes mountains. Alpacas produce very fine wool. Llamas are used for transport.

Goats, sheep, cattle and donkeys are not as well adapted to the desert as camels are. They need water more often and cannot walk so far from the wells and waterholes. However, they still live far longer without drinking than humans. Camels, in particular, continue eating during the heat of the day, even when they are thirsty.

SPREADING DESERT

All over the world, the desert is spreading into the fertile lands beyond. The climate has changed many times over the centuries. Rock paintings made thousands of years ago in caves in the south east of Algeria show that giraffes, elephant and rhinoceros must have lived in what are now desert areas. Only 160 years ago, a French explorer wrote of thick woods in the central Nile region and noises of lions roaring. Today, that kind of life has disappeared and the desert has taken over.

These regions have never received much rain. Gradually, over the past century, the land has turned into desert because the number of people and domestic animals has increased. So much of the grass has been eaten that there is now no vegetation to hold up the water. So the rain runs in torrents off the surface of the land, and down the *wadis* before there is time for it to sink into the soil. In times of drought when food was scarce people have had to cut down the trees for firewood in order to keep alive. Much of the Sahel savannah has been invaded by the Sahara during the last twenty years. The same thing is happening around the Indian desert. When there are too many people and not enough water, the land almost always becomes a desert.

Goats can strip an area of land bare of all vegetation. They eat practically anything and are even able to climb trees and eat the leaves. Goats and sheep are a cause of soil loss. Over a period of time, animal tracks break the surface of the desert soil. When the rain falls, the tracks form gulleys down which the soil is washed away. If properly managed in the right environment, goats are valuable domestic animals. However, where the desert has already spread for a variety of reasons, including human mistakes, goats can cause even more damage. ▶

This picture shows what happens when too many people, with too many goats and sheep, live on the edge of the desert. The desert extends into their homeland. If there is a drought too, then the people starve. Many people, especially children and the very old, die every day in Ethiopia, Chad, and throughout the Sahel savannah zone of Africa.

Oasis Expansion

Where there is water, the desert can be extremely fertile. The sun shines every day, so plants grow quickly. Several crops can be harvested each year. One way of halting the spread of desert, is to increase the oases so that they provide more food. Oases whose waters come from springs have usually been fully developed for a long time.

Irrigation

Throughout the world's deserts, new wells are being dug and old wells deepened. In the past, water had to be raised by a goatskin bucket attached to a rawhide rope, pulled up by a donkey or camel. Another way to get the water up was to use a *shadouf*. This consisted of a goatskin bucket tied to one end of a wooden beam which rocked like a seesaw. The other end was balanced by a bag of rocks. This lightened the work of the person who had to lift the full goatskins and tip them into the irrigation ditch. Where the water lay further below the surface, a water wheel could be used. The shadouf and the water wheel were invented in prehistoric times, and are still in use today.

None of these devices brings up water very quickly, so they do not take too much water. Today they are being replaced everywhere by motor pumps and, indeed, are becoming scarce. Much more water can be pumped by a "donkey engine", so now the level of water in the wells is sinking all the time.

Aswan High Dam

The valley of the Nile is the world's largest oasis. Annual floods have always been a cause for rejoicing. These flood waters flow down the Blue Nile from Ethiopia. They are colored deep brown because they contain so much fine mud or silt. Nile silt is extremely fertile.

▲ A plantation of young palms in the valley of the River Jordan. This new oasis has been constructed artificially, and provides a livelihood for many settlers.

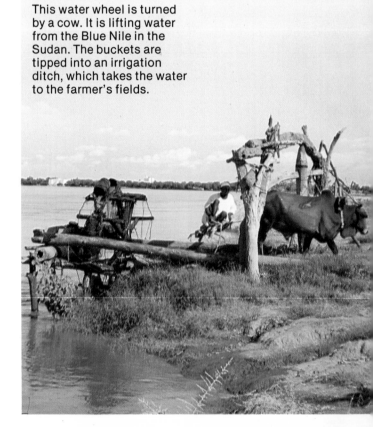

This water wheel is turned by a cow. It is lifting water from the Blue Nile in the Sudan. The buckets are tipped into an irrigation ditch, which takes the water to the farmer's fields.

◀ A modern agricultural scheme at Kufra in Libya. The pipes take water to overhead sprinklers. This prevents the soil getting waterlogged and salty. However, the water comes from deep wells and will not last indefinitely.

As the flood waters settled, the silt was deposited on the banks of the river. Then the farmers of Egypt and the Sudan planted their crops. They grew peas, beans, tomatoes, wheat, maize, rice, onions and alfalfa for their sheep and cows.

Since the High Dam was built at Aswan, the cultivated area beside the Nile has been greatly increased. Egypt can now provide enough wheat for itself and it can also export rice. The water passing through the sluices of the dam drives turbines which generate 10 billion kilowatt hours of electricity per year. The Nile silt no longer enriches the land. Instead, a large chemical industry has been set up to produce artificial fertilizers.

However, the dam has also caused problems. The rich fishing industry off the Nile delta has been destroyed because nutrients no longer flow into the Mediterranean. There has been a considerable increase in bilharzia disease. So the great dam has brought disadvantages as well as advantages to Egypt by increasing the area of oasis.

Irrigation

Since earliest times, people who live beside the great desert rivers of the world have drawn water to irrigate their crops. In Egypt traditional means of irrigation such as the shadouf and the water wheel are still being used in some places to take water into the fields of the Nile valley.

The ancient qanat is another means of irrigation which can still be found in Iran and throughout the Middle East. The qanat is a sloping tunnel, leading from a well to a low lying area where crops are grown. Water from the well flows freely, but slowly through the tunnel to the irrigated area. There are 3,000 miles of qanats in the Sahara alone. Many of them are now clogged. The qanats were dug mainly by slave labor, and very few new ones are being made today.

▲ A dam across the River Euphrates in Syria. Large dams provide water for irrigation throughout the year. The force of running water drives turbines. These produce electricity for homes and to power factories.

▲ A qanat system coming to the surface at Turpan Oasis, in Iran. The water is brought underground along a tunnel from a well or spring at the foot of distant mountains.

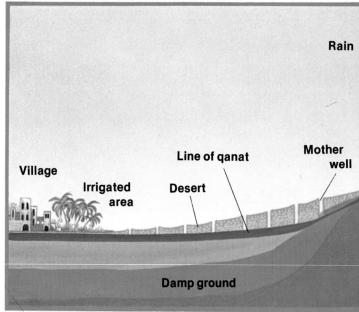

▲ Rain falling on a mountain range is taken by an underground qanat to an oasis. The earth from the tunnel has been brought to the surface through the vertical shafts.

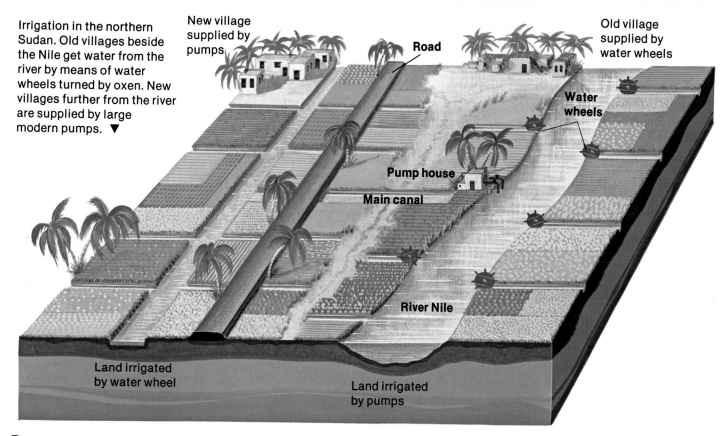

Irrigation in the northern Sudan. Old villages beside the Nile get water from the river by means of water wheels turned by oxen. New villages further from the river are supplied by large modern pumps. ▼

New village supplied by pumps

Road

Old village supplied by water wheels

Water wheels

Pump house

Main canal

River Nile

Land irrigated by water wheel

Land irrigated by pumps

Pumps

In western Texas, over 65,000 wells pump water to irrigate vast areas of land. The fossil water they draw is in limited supply and the wells are not being refilled. The level of the water has dropped at a rate of about 3 feet per year during the last thirty years. At Kufra, in Libya, water is brought up from a depth of 1,500 feet to irrigate 125,000 acres. This is very expensive, but up to 15 crops of alfalfa can be grown every year. At the same time, the water level is dropping, and date palms in the oasis are beginning to die. Farming projects in lower California are sometimes based on wells that are not expected to last more than 10-15 years.

Dams

The largest irrigation schemes draw their water from dams across rivers. The water is held back in reservoirs. From these reservoirs huge areas of desert land are irrigated. At the same time, dams supply hydroelectric power to the region. There are dams across the Nile, Indus, Volga, Don, Ural, Tigris, Euphrates, Amu Darya, Hwang Ho, Colorado, Snake, Rio Grande and Orange Rivers. You might think that dams and irrigation schemes could solve the problems of the deserts. The main problem is shortage of water but waterlogging and salinization of the soil, also have to be tackled.

Waterlogging and salinization

It is not at all easy to irrigate desert land without eventually making it impossible for plants to grow ther, except where sprinkler or drip irrigation is used. First of all, the land has to be completely flat. If there is the slightest hollow, the water will collect in it, leaving the rest of the ground dry and barren. Even when the land is absolutely flat, it is still very difficult to let in just enough water to soak the soil, without letting in too much.

If too much water is pumped onto the fields, the ground may become waterlogged. Because it is so flat, the water cannot run away. So the soil easily becomes waterlogged and crops will not grow. Even when the right amount of water is supplied, evaporation by the hot desert sun draws salts out of the earth. These salts clog up the surface soil and prevent plants from growing. Unless the soil lets surplus water drain through it, both waterlogging and salinization may occur.

Over one third of irrigated land in the Indus valley has been lost to agriculture through waterlogging and salinization. In China, one fifth of all irrigation schemes have failed for the same reason. There are similar problems in Jordan, Syria, Morocco, the U.S.A., Australia, Brazil, Haiti and many other Third World countries.

Improved Land Use

There are many ways in which the use of water can be improved. Water can be applied to growing crops by overhead sprinklers. These save precious water. They reduce the risk of waterlogging and the accumulation of salt.

Hydroponics

Another way of saving water is to grow plants in sand in which plastic pipes with holes in them are buried. Water containing fertilizers is pumped through the pipes once or twice daily. This leaks through the holes and irrigates the roots of the plants without wetting the surface of the sand. In this way, little water is wasted through evaporation. This method is called hydroponics. The use of hydroponics to grow tomatoes, for instance, requires much less water than surface irrigation.

Run-off irrigation

Most of the world's desert land is much too far from any rivers to be able to get water from them. In many places, too, there is either no water beneath the surface or there is salt. So it is no use digging wells. The only thing to do is to plant crops that grow quickly and do not need much water.

These crops have to be planted immediately after the rain has fallen. It helps if the flow of water down hillsides is directed toward the flat places where the crops are to be grown. This is known as "run-off" irrigation. At the same time, if this dry land farming is carried out too intensively at the desert's edge, the desert will spread. Intensive dryland farming was the cause of much of the spread of the Sahara into the Sahel.

The greatest desert dunes move slowly along, driven by the prevailing wind. They can be held in place by planting trees on them. If this were not done, the dunes would engulf the oases and plantations that lie in their paths.

▲ In this greenhouse in the Middle East cucumbers are grown using a method called hydroponics. It only takes a few weeks to grow cucumbers and tomatoes that way.

▲ Trees are standing in run-off water after a rainstorm in Israel. Rainwater trickles down the valley and waters the farmland. This method of irrigating trees is called run-off farming.

Preventing soil loss

Permanent vegetation can manage to survive on sand dunes, provided that at least 15 inches of rain falls each year. The surfaces of the dunes have to be held in place first. This can be done by spraying them with a mixture of oil and synthetic rubber. Acacia and eucalyptus tree seedlings are then planted. When these have taken a firm hold their roots get water stored below the surface of the dunes from one wet season to the next. As they grow, the trees prevent sand and dust from blowing away. Dead leaves get into the soil and help to bind it together. The Trans-Caspian railway from the Caspian Sea to Samarkand could not be built until the dunes had been held in place with bushes. This means of stabilizing dunes is a useful way of preventing desert expansion.

Everything that stops the soil being blown or washed away by wind or water is for the good. Plants also help to break up the soil so that rain water runs into it. It is no use planting grass or tree seedlings unless they can be protected from sheep and goats. So, new plantations have to be fenced in, which is very expensive. Poor people, and the governments of developing countries cannot afford to do this.

Tourism and camping

Tourism brings in money but tourists can do a great deal of harm when they drive their cars and trailers off the roads in desert areas. Except in areas with moving dunes, the desert soil is often fixed by microscopic plants. A crust, formed by threads of algae, fungi, and lichens, hardens the surface and increases its roughness. When this crust is broken up by car wheels, the soil blows away. Herbs and grasses are killed when they are run over. Shrubs and trees die when the soil blows away and their roots are exposed.

Exploitation of Minerals

Desert countries tend to be rich if they have oil and poor if they do not have any. Even in countries rich in oil, not everyone benefits from the wealth it brings. The richest of desert countries have poor people living in them. In Kuwait, in the Middle East, people earn more money per person than in any other country in the world. Yet there are slums outside Kuwait City in which very poor people live. They have little hope of ever getting proper houses.

The most obvious riches of barren lands, and the most desired are deposits of oil and valuable minerals. Oil can be sold to other countries to obtain currency to pay for imports and development projects. Kuwait and Saudi Arabia have some of the best equipped hospitals in the world. Oil and natural gas can be used to turn salt water into fresh water. Only countries with enough money and the means to exploit oil can afford to do this.

▲ Oil money has brought the 20th century to the Arab countries of the Middle East. Today, the ancient cultures of the people still exist alongside modern amenities and technology.

▲ Open-cast coal mining in Western Australia. Many desert regions contain rich deposits of minerals. In Third World countries, these can be used to provide money for the poor people that live in them, or to pay for development schemes.

◄ Oil has provided great wealth to the peoples of many desert regions. The wells are capped and the oil conveyed across the desert in huge pipes. At the coast, it is either refined or loaded directly into the tankers. These take the crude oil to refineries in Europe or America. Wealth has also brought important changes to people's lives. For instance many Bedouins who used to live a nomadic life settled down on new farms or came to live in town. However, the move from a tent to a house has caused problems in some families. Often, relatives no longer live close together in the same house and so family ties are weakened.

Many of the world's largest oil deposits have been found in desert countries: Arabia, Iraq, Iran, Algeria, Libya and comparatively less in south-western U.S.A. (see map page 43).

Mining

Some extremely rich mines are scattered throughout the deserts of the world. They contain minerals such as diamonds, silver, iron ore, lead, bauxite, gypsum, uranium, nitrates and phosphates. Over three-quarters of the world's gold is mined in South Africa, Namibia and the U.S.S.R. New discoveries have recently been made in Australia. The world's largest deposit of borax lies in the Mojave desert.

The exploitation of minerals is a hard and difficult job anywhere in the world. If the deposits are in remote desert regions it may cost too much to transport them to where they are needed. Work in desert mines is usually highly paid. Food and water, as well as facilities for recreation and leisure, have to be brought to the miners. And they need to be sent all the way home for their vacations. Even so, in the iron ore mines of northwestern Australia, each job is filled by up to five different workers each year.

Many types of mining operation require large amounts of water. This is not available in the desert unless it is transported by pipeline. After two years of droughts, water had to be brought by rail to the mining town of Broken Hill, in Australia. The town's 27,000 inhabitants needed eight train loads of water every day. Then, the last train, on January 17, 1946, was derailed by a flash flood! The costs of operating a desert mine may prove so great that it is not economical to do so unless mineral deposits are very rich.

Some minerals exist in the desert just because of the dryness of the soil. These minerals would dissolve in rain water. They include borax, rock salt, gypsum and nitrates. Nitrates and phosphates are valuable fertilizers.

The Future

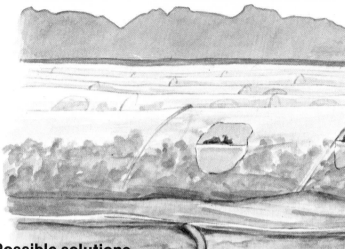

Although the desert may be a howling wilderness, nations throughout the ages have constantly been fighting over it. During the last ten years, most of the Middle East and North African countries have been engaged in wars. Some historians think that wars between peoples of the desert are really conflicts over the resources of the cultivated lands beside them.

The human population of the deserts and of the barren lands surrounding them is increasing all the time. During the past thirty years, modern drugs and medicine have helped to keep people alive. Many new wells have been dug so that the grazing areas could be increased. Then the number of goats and sheep increased still more. As more animals grazed on the same piece of land, the grass did not have time to grow back fast enough. So the desert spread still further, as it did in the Sahel.

If a poor farmer in the Sahel has three good years for every seven years of drought, what can he do? He has no money, no bank account. So he invests in another goat to give him and his family more milk during the next drought. So even more land is turned into desert.

Better planning

If no family had more than two children, the population of the world would probably decline. Perhaps one way of reducing the increase in the number of people who live in the desert is to educate them so that they do not have so many children. However, family planning advice is not easy to offer to people who have suffered from starvation as they have in the Sahel drought over the past twenty years. When people see children die one after the other, they tend to want more children in the hope that one or two may survive.

Possible solutions

As things are at present, the future looks bleak. Nevertheless the desert could probably support a few more people than it does now, without expanding. A combination of better use of the land and family planning could, in the long run help to solve the problem, but there will undoubtedly be much more suffering before this has been achieved. How can the barren lands be made to produce more, without making the desert spread further? A number of possibilities can be suggested. Many small farming projects make a better use of the land than fewer larger ones.

▲ The saiga antelope thrives in the deserts of the U.S.S.R. Large herds provide enough meat and leather to support many people.

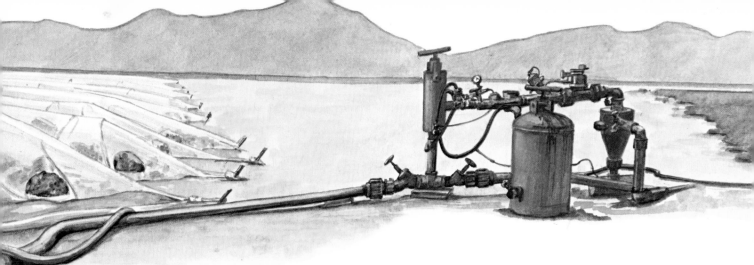

This huge dish aerial is the desert's communication link with other parts of the world. In many barren countries, satellite ground stations track the passage of artificial satellites across the skies. ▶

▲ Here vegetables and fruit are grown under plastic sheets, in the desert of Israel. Water from pipes is used to irrigate them.

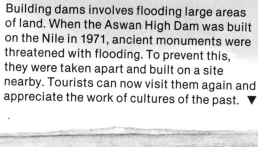

Building dams involves flooding large areas of land. When the Aswan High Dam was built on the Nile in 1971, ancient monuments were threatened with flooding. To prevent this, they were taken apart and built on a site nearby. Tourists can now visit them again and appreciate the work of cultures of the past. ▼

In the past, the World Bank and some governments have supported big projects. Many of these have resulted in enormous disasters. Large areas should not be used for the same type of land use. There should be many small and varied agricultural schemes, both dryland and irrigated. Herding ought to be limited to small herds of sheep and goats. Nomadism should be encouraged to avoid overgrazing. Satellite photographs could be used to find out where rain has fallen, and radio messages sent to tell the nomads which way to go. Crops which use less water can be produced by plant breeding.

Research into new irrigation schemes may also offer new solutions. Ambitious plans to change the course of rivers in the Volga basin and around the Aral Sea will increase the farmland area in barren parts of European Russia. These are some of the ways in which a better use of the desert could be made for the long term benefit of the people who live there.

Books and Places

Books to read

Deserts of the World (Watson) Philomel, N.Y.C., New York

Desert People (Kent) Warwick, N.Y.C., New York

Desert (Leopold) Time-Life, N.Y.C., New York

Soviet Deserts (St. George) Time-Life, N.Y.C., New York

Deserts (Porsell) Childrens Press, Chicago, Illinois

Finding Out About Earth (Usborne) Usborne/Hayes, Tulsa, Oklahoma

McGraw-Hill Encyclopaedia of Environmental Science, McGraw-Hill, N.Y.C., New York

Great Explorations

The desert has always attracted explorers. Many of the earliest expeditions, like those of the Spanish conquerors to the deserts of North and South America, went in search of new lands and gold. More recent expeditions have traveled in search in knowledge.

1822-1823 Hugh Clapperton, Walter Oudney and Dixon Denham crossed the Sahara from Tripoli and were the first Europeans to see Lake Chad. Later they separated and Clapperton pushed on to Kano.

1853-1854 In 1853, Sir Richard Burton went on pilgrimage to Mecca. The following year he explored the interior of Somalia and later, with J.H. Speke, explored the sources of the Nile. He is chiefly remembered for his translation of the book *Arabian Nights*.

1850-1856 Heinrich Barth, a pioneer explorer of the Sahara traveled from Tripoli to Kano and Timbuctoo, and back by way of Lake Chad and Mourzouk in central Libya.

1860-1861 Robert O'Hara Burke led an expedition into the interior of Australia which ended tragically. Burke and his two companions died in the desert.

1913-1914 Gertrude Bell traveled from Damascus into the interior of Arabia.

1927-1929 Dame Freya Stark traveled in Lebanon and Syria on a donkey, and then explored the wild and remote parts of Persia. She wrote many books on her travels in the desert.

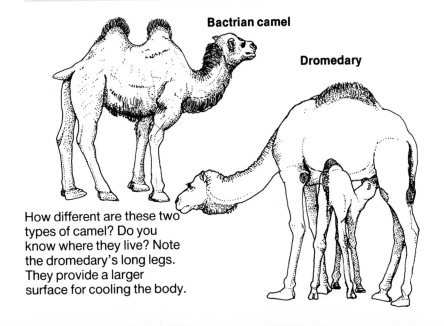

Bactrian camel

Dromedary

How different are these two types of camel? Do you know where they live? Note the dromedary's long legs. They provide a larger surface for cooling the body.

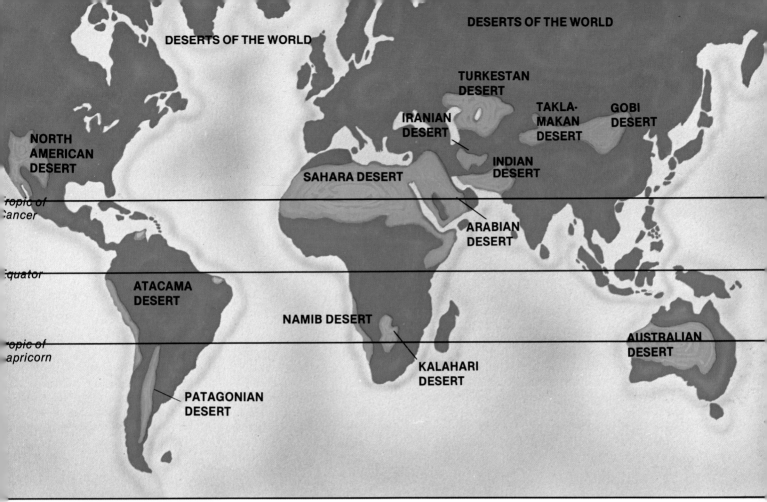

DESERTS OF THE WORLD

Deserts of the World	Square Miles	Mineral Resources
Sahara Desert	3,500,000	Oil, uranium, iron, nitrates
Australian Desert	1,300,000	Coal, iron, diamonds, lead
Turkestan Desert	750,000	
Arabian Desert	1,000,000	Oil, bauxite
Great American Desert (including the Great Basin, Mojave, Sonoran and Chihuahuan Deserts of south western North America)	500,000	Bauxite, silver, copper, lead
Patagonian Desert (Argentina)	260,000	
Thar Desert (India)	230,000	
Kalahari and Namib Deserts (South West Africa)	220,000	Gold, uranium, diamonds
Takla Makan Desert including the Gobi Desert (from western China to Mongolia)	200,000	Silver, diamonds
Iranian Desert (Persia)	150,000	
Atacama Desert (Peru and Chile)	140,000	Copper, nitrates, phosphates

Word List

Algae Simple, primitive flowerless plants, sometimes growing in desert soil.

Arroyo Spanish name for a desert water course that is dry for most of the year.

Bauxite A clay from which aluminium can be extracted.

Bilharzia Disease caused by the presence in the body of blood flukes. It affects humans, horses, donkeys, camels, sheep and cattle.

Boron A non-metallic element which occurs in nature in the form of borax.

Camel spiders Spider-like predatory arachnids, related to scorpions, with segmented bodies and relatively enormous jaws. Non-poisonous.

Delta An area of land where the mouth of a river or stream fans out. It is formed by deposits of sediment.

Donkey engine A small steam or gas driven pump.

Ephemeral A plant which completes its life cycle in a very short time.

Erg Expanse of sand dunes or sand sea.

Evaporation The process of change into water vapor.

Fluke Flattened, parasitic worm.

Fossil Water Water trapped underneath the Earth's crust during the Ice Ages.

Fungi Simple colorless parasitic plants whose filaments are often found in soil.

Gypsum Crystalline compound of calcium used in the manufacture of plaster of Paris.

Hammada Rocky desert. In an extreme form, hammada is completely bare rock.

Irrigation Artificial means of watering the land.

Lichen Flowerless plants formed by a mixture of algae and fungi.

Malaria A fever caused by infection with parasites spread by the bite of certain mosquitoes.

Monsoon Climatic type of India, much of Southeast Asia and the Sahara, with maximum rainfall in summer.

Nomadism Way of life practiced by desert people, such as Bedouins. They live in regions where the irregular rainfall forces them to move with their herds from one area, in which rain has fallen, to another.

Oasis A place in the desert where there is fresh water, allowing settlements and agriculture to be established.

Plateau A high but mainly flat land region.

Qanat A long tunnel to conduct water from an underground source to a cultivated area, made by sinking a number of shafts and joining them with short lengths of tunnel.

Reg Name given to stony desert.

Reservoir An artificial lake usually retained by a dam across a river.

Sahel The belt of dry, barren savannah fringing the southern and northern edge of the Sahara desert.

Sandfly fever Acute disease due to infection conveyed by the bite of a sandfly.

Scale insects Flattened sap sucking bugs that cause damage to plants.

Satellite A craft launched into space and put into orbit around the earth. Satellites can be used to scan desert vegetation, cloud formations etc.

Shadouf A method of lifting water.

Sheik Arab chief or leader.

Slit Fine bits of soil and rock powder

Spring A flow of water from the ground.

Turbine Engine driven by flowing water or steam directed onto a tube or wheel carrying curved vanes which cause it to rotate.

Vermin Harmful, unwanted animal.

Wadi Desert watercourse, dry except after rainfall.

Well A hold in the ground through which water or oil are raised to the surface.

Index